Jacob's Ladder

Reading Comprehension Program

Grade

5

Student Workbook Short Stories

Contributing Editors:
Joyce VanTassel-Baska,
Tamra Stambaugh,
Kimberley L. Chandler

Contributing Authors:
Heather French,
Paula Ginsburgh,
Tamra Stambaugh,
Joyce VanTassel-Baska

William & Mary
School of Education
CENTER FOR GIFTED EDUCATION

William & Mary
School of Education
Center for Gifted Education
P.O. Box 8795
Williamsburg, VA 23187

First published in 2017 by Prufrock Press Inc.

Published 2021 by Routledge
605 Third Avenue, New York, NY 10017
2 Park Square, Milton Park, Abingdon, Oxon OX14 4RN

Routledge is an imprint of the Taylor & Francis Group, an informa business

Copyright ©2017, Center for Gifted Education, William & Mary

All rights reserved. No part of this book may be reprinted or reproduced or utilised in any form or by any electronic, mechanical, or other means, now known or hereafter invented, including photocopying and recording, or in any information storage or retrieval system, without permission in writing from the publishers.

Notice:
Product or corporate names may be trademarks or registered trademarks, and are used only for identification and explanation without intent to infringe.

Edited by Lacy Compton

Cover and layout design by Allegra Denbo

ISBN-13: 978-1-61821-736-3

NEW YORK AND LONDON

Table of Contents

A Plentiful Harvest

By Jenny Li

The coffee beans and cacao pods fell off the plants. The nopales shriveled into child-palm-sized prunes. And the tomatillos evaporated into nothingness, leaving behind only the paper-thin husks, soft green and delicate like Chinese lanterns.

The villagers stopped walking to the market and instead sat, defeated, in the shades of their houses, their shirts stained with perspiration. The once-plentiful kapok trees had turned brittle and drooped toward the soil, craning for a single drop of water. The faint mist was a remainder of the haze that had once draped the surrounding jungle.

By the morning of the 30th day of the drought, there was no water in the stream. By the afternoon, white spores were floating in the air, making the town look like it was covered in pillow feathers. The dust had risen into whirlwinds as high as Jéssica's waist.

Jéssica's stand was pitiful—less than a dozen squash and onions lined the table, lacking their vibrant yellows. They had shrunk almost into themselves, creating cavities and dents that she was ashamed to bring out into the stand. The onions were almost falling apart, and the customers could clearly see the dried-out beige insides of the once-flaxen skin. They barely glanced at her display, and Jéssica returned to her home with a weathered bag slung on her shoulder, holding all the produce she started with, with the exception of a single shriveled squash that her neighbor purchased out of sympathy.

Later that night, sitting under a sky heavily blanketed with stars, Jéssica slurped her bowl of pozole, recounting the day's meager profits. She had thrown out the other vegetables that she had tried to sell—though it seemed impossible, they had worsened from their already-shriveled state to a shade of burnt, ashen dark green. She could not imagine what was to come in the following days, or weeks, living in this always-hungry, never-satisfied way.

A stream of tears rolled off her cheek into her dirt-cracked palm, and she scoffed at the irony that her tears—the water she had plenty of—was the only water source that she could not use. She felt the weight in her hand increase and watched the cupped pool of tears gradually swell into a powder blue pillow, almost the size of her palm. Gleaming in the light, the small melon held more than an entire day's portion of water, encapsulated by a rubber-like skin. Jéssica opened up the lip of the encasing and drank eagerly. With the next balloon of water, she washed her face and hands, and then used the next few to dampen the soil around the dried out geranium pots hanging on either side of the front door.

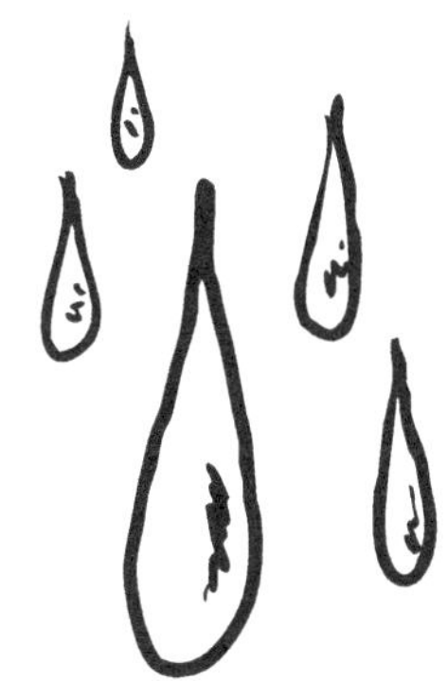

~

The commotion of the shoppers huddled around Jéssica's stand made the rest of the farmer's market look like an empty lot. The shouting and shoving alone would have made her uncomfortable, but so near the balloons, the rough behavior was now a threat to her delicate produce carefully placed into the apple crates and shallow boxes she was able to repurpose from her failed farming days.

"¡Muchacha, dame una docena de estos globos de agua!"

From the heavy-set aunties in house dresses and wide huaraches, to the young mothers with sticky, sleeping infants strapped to them in colorful yards of fabric, they all yelled in her direction, and she did her best to serve them in some sort of order, trying to remember who had been there first and who was pushing their way forward with elbows and teeth baring.

The next Saturday at the market was more of the same—people yelling, shoving creased bills and jingling coins into Jéssica's hand—the water balloons glistening in the relentless noon sun in their prime spot on the vinyl floral tablecloth covering the vegetable stall. Jéssica was quietly happy, though tiredness and tear trails stamped her face in red blotches and dark under-eye circles. She had spent the whole night bending over chopped onions, improvising, as the tears wouldn't come, for she was well-fed and happy now! What was there to cry about?

~

Already the following Saturday, the traffic around Jéssica's stand had decreased. That morning, little Luciana, the daughter of Jéssica's second cousin, who lived on the other end of the village, woke up sneezing Guyana anchovies into her parents' overjoyed arms, holding buckets and crates and anything else they could find. Now, the village, having quenched their thirst but not yet their hunger, circled the family's array of receptacles full to the brim of shiny, slippery fish the size of Jéssica's forefinger.

Jéssica sold about a dozen of her tear balloons and left early that day.

The next Saturday, her side of the market was almost completely empty—even the other vendors had abandoned their stands for the rumors that Antonio's deep waves of laughter in response to Abuela Ada's wisecrack was manifesting in the brightest ripples of pima cotton that the villagers had ever seen. Antonio's laugh had been known across the village and was welcomed at all the fiestas and bodas, but now the bell-like reverberations coming from Antonio's belly were coming into this world as beautiful folds and swirls quivering in the heat. Abuela Ada's granddaughters had set to work on sewing together vibrant guyaberas lined with the designs of sprouting carnations and orange-red sunsets. Before long, the village resembled a blooming garden, with its residents, clothed in the most beautiful creations, sashaying and swishing up and down the main square in visible enjoyment over their own resplendent beauty.

~

The balloons lay limp in the flat tray that Jéssica had washed behind the house the night before. Dozens of shoppers walked by the stand, grazing their fingers on the latex, leaving greasy fingerprints on the blue sheen.

The people were happy, their thirst quenched, their mouths fed, and bodies clothed. Jéssica could not have known that miraculous harvest, which her tears had started, would solve all of their problems. She felt an overwhelming urge to cry.

Note. Originally published in *Creative Kids* magazine, Fall 2016. Reprinted with permission by Prufrock Press.

A PLENTIFUL HARVEST

Consequences and Implications

A3 Suppose another drought comes to the village. What are some of the potential implications?

Cause and Effect

A2 What caused the villagers to stop walking to the market? What effects did it have?

Sequencing

A1 List the six most important events in the story in order.

Generalizations

B3 What generalizations can you make about the market?

Classifications

B2 Classify the details in your list into categories.

Details

B1 List all the details you can find that the author provides about the market.

The Elves and the Cobbler

By Jacob Grimm and Wilhelm Grimm

There was once a cobbler, who worked very hard and was very honest, but still he could not earn enough to live upon; and at last all he had in the world was gone, save just leather enough to make one pair of shoes.

Then he cut his leather out, all ready to make up the next day, meaning to rise early in the morning to his work. His conscience was clear and his heart light amidst all his troubles; so he went peaceably to bed, left all his cares to Heaven, and soon fell asleep. In the morning after he had said his prayers, he sat himself down to his work; when, to his great wonder, there stood the shoes all ready made upon the table. The good man knew not what to say or think at such an odd thing happening. He looked at the workmanship; there was not one false stitch in the whole job; all was so neat and true, that it was quite a masterpiece.

The same day a customer came in, and the shoes suited him so well that he willingly paid a price higher than usual for them; and the poor shoemaker, with the money, bought leather enough to make two pair more. In the evening he cut out the work, and went to bed early, that he might get up and begin betimes next day, but he was saved all the trouble, for when he got up in the morning the work was done ready to his hand. Soon in came buyers, who paid him handsomely for his goods, so that he bought leather enough for four pair more. He cut out the work again over-night and found it done in the morning, as before, and so it went on for some time: what was got ready in the evening was always done by daybreak, and the good man soon became thriving and well off again.

One evening, about Christmas time, as he and his wife were sitting over the fire chatting together, he said to her, "I should like to sit up and watch to-night, that we may see who it is that comes and does my work for me." The wife liked the thought; so they left a light burning, and hid themselves in a corner of the room, behind a curtain that was hung up there, and watched what should happen.

As soon as it was midnight, there came in two little naked dwarfs; and they sat themselves upon the shoemaker's bench, took up all the work that was cut out, and began to ply with their little fingers, stitching and rapping and tapping away at such a rate, that the shoemaker was all wonder, and could not take his eyes off them. And on they went, till the job was quite done, and the shoes stood ready for use upon the table. This was long before daybreak, and then they bustled away as quick as lightning.

The next day the wife said to the shoemaker, "These little wights have made us rich, and we ought to be thankful to them, and do them a good turn if we can. I am quite sorry to see them run about as they do; and indeed it is not very decent, for they have nothing upon their backs to keep off the cold. I'll tell you what, I will make each of them a shirt, and a coat and waistcoat, and a pair of pantaloons into the bargain; and do you make each of them a little pair of shoes."

The thought pleased the good cobbler very much; and one evening, when all the things were ready, they laid them on the table, instead of the work that they used to cut out, and then went and hid themselves, to watch what the little elves would do.

About midnight in they came, dancing and skipping, hopped round the room, and then went to sit down to their work as usual, but when they saw the clothes lying for them, they laughed and chuckled, and seemed mightily delighted.

Then they dressed themselves in the twinkling of an eye, and danced and capered and sprang about, as merry as could be, till at last they danced out at the door, and away over the green.

The good couple saw them no more, but every thing went well with them from that time forward, as long as they lived.

THE ELVES AND THE COBBLER

Consequences and Implications

A3 How might the cobbler's life have been different if the elves had not helped him?

Cause and Effect

A2 What caused the cobbler to become so poor? Support your answer.

Sequencing

A1 List the seven main events of the story in order.

Main Idea, Theme, or Concept

C3 Concept: In what ways does the author address the concept of kindness?

Inference

C2 Could the cobbler have been successful without the assistance of the elves? Explain your answer.

Literary Elements

C1 Describe the cobbler's personality. Support your answer.

Intense

By Audrey Lai

I backed into a corner, sweat pouring down my face and neck. I tried to find an opening that I could squeeze out of. No such luck. Suddenly, a shadow closed in; a menacing figure smelling of rotten bananas and Glacier Freeze Gatorade loomed over me. Well, if I was going to go down, I might as well go down fighting.

With a loud battle cry, I threw myself at him and put my remaining power into a kick that landed on his head, just above his ear. Stunned, he took a step back, his hand clutching the spot where my foot made contact. I kicked again, this time striking his ribs, but he recovered easily.

I paused, trying to anticipate his movements, but he was fast. The next thing I knew, he was kicking and punching, whirling about like a tornado. I moved in cautiously, one step at a time. He paused for a second, trying to catch his breath, and I took the opportunity.

I kicked repeatedly, aiming for his head, but he was better than I gave him credit for. Most of my blows missed him, except for one that caught him on the stomach. He doubled over in pain. I stepped up even closer, a risky move. Suddenly, he straightened up and threw a hard jab that missed me.

While I was still surprised, he kicked me harder than I had ever felt before. He crouched, preparing to let loose a kick that could surely knock me out. I had no choice. If I wanted to win the fight, I had to do it.

I ran up to him and pressed my body against his. Stunned, he tried to kick, but only managed to knee the air next to me. He tried and missed again. This was it. When he kicked for the third time, I punched him hard, and there was a loud smack as my fist made contact with his chest.

Off balance, he stumbled backward, arms flailing wildly as he struggled to regain his balance. I saw my chance, and I took it. Gathering my energy, I released a kick that hit him on his left ear, and down he went. I looked down at him, his face a mixture of pain and disbelief. I paused for a second, pondering my choices. Sighing, I reached down and grasped his hand tightly, pulling him to his feet. Boy, was he heavy!

At that moment, the bell rang, signaling the end of the match.

"Back to position!" barked the referee. We stood, about an arm's length apart, and my opponent glared at me.

"Attention!" yelled the referee. We immediately straightened up, backs straight, arms and legs together.

The referee shouted, "Bow!"

I bowed down low, trying to show good sportsmanship, but my opponent didn't care. He barely lowered his head. "And the winner is . . . " the referee announced. "Joshua!"

"Yeah!" he exploded. "I won! In your face!"

I blinked back tears, and my coach came over to me, his steely expression unusually soft. "Stay strong, Audrey. Win or lose, you tried your best, and I'm so proud of you."

I nodded solemnly. "Now go get your medal," he said, showing a rare smile and patting me on the back.

I felt a burst of pride as I skipped over to the scoring area, where Joshua had just taken his place in the winner's box. I stood next to him, beaming. The referee took his spot in the grandstand. "May I have your attention, please? The final score for the Taekwondo Junior Category Championships is . . . Joshua, 8, and Audrey . . . 7!"

I gasped. It was beyond anything I had ever imagined. I had only lost by one point! The referee walked up to me. "Stupendous job, Audrey!" he said, as he hung the medal around my neck. "Thank you!" I replied.

He grasped my hand firmly in a brief handshake, then assumed his position in the grandstand again. "Congratulations to our winners, Joshua and Audrey!" the referee shouted into the microphone. I grinned. I didn't care that I had lost.

Note. Originally published in *Creative Kids* magazine, Summer 2016. Reprinted with permission by Prufrock Press.

INTENSE

Main Idea, Theme, or Concept

C3 Theme: Identify the theme of this short story in one sentence.

Inference

C2 Could the author have won the competition? What evidence supports your answer?

Literary Elements

C1 The author of the story experiences many emotions during the competition. What emotions does she experience? How do you know?

Creative Synthesis

D3 On another sheet of paper, write another version of the essay from the narrator's opponent's point of view.

Summarizing

D2 In five sentences or fewer, summarize the author's competition experience.

Paraphrasing

D1 In your own words, paraphrase this sentence from the story: "Well, if I was going to go down, I might as well go down fighting."

The Real Princess

By Hans Christian Andersen

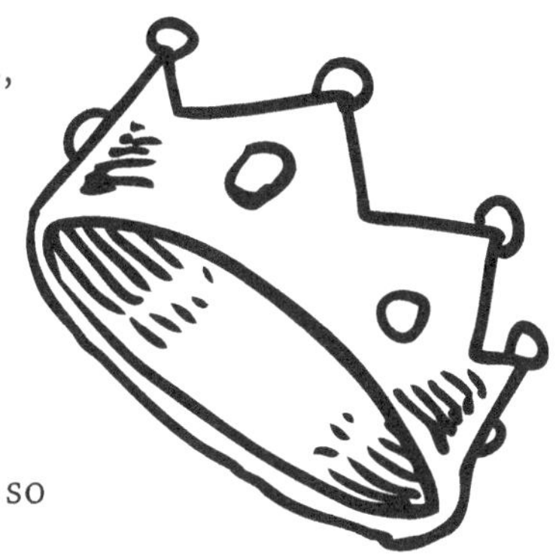

There was once a Prince who wished to marry a Princess, but then she must be a real Princess. He travelled all over the world in hopes of finding such a lady, but there was always something wrong. Princesses he found in plenty, but whether they were real Princesses it was impossible for him to decide, for now one thing, now another, seemed to him not quite right about the ladies. At last he returned to his palace quite cast down, because he wished so much to have a real Princess for his wife.

One evening a fearful tempest arose; it thundered and lightened, and the rain poured down from the sky in torrents; besides, it was as dark as pitch. All at once there was heard a violent knocking at the door, and the old King, the Prince's father, went out himself to open it.

It was a Princess who was standing outside the door. What with the rain and the wind, she was in a sad condition: the water trickled down from her hair, and her clothes clung to her body. She said she was a real Princess.

"Ah, we shall soon see that!" thought the old Queen-mother; however, she said not a word of what she was going to do, but went quietly into the bedroom, took all the bed-clothes off the bed, and put three little peas on the bedstead. She then laid twenty mattresses one upon another over the three peas, and put twenty feather-beds over the mattresses.

Upon this bed the Princess was to pass the night.

The next morning she was asked how she had slept. "Oh, very badly indeed!" she replied. "I have scarcely closed my eyes the whole night through. I do not know what was in my bed, but I had something hard under me, and am all over black and blue. It has hurt me so much!"

Now it was plain that the lady must be a real Princess, since she had been able to feel the three little peas through the twenty mattresses and twenty feather-beds. None but a real Princess could have had such a delicate sense of feeling.

The Prince accordingly made her his wife, being now convinced that he had found a real Princess. The three peas were, however, put into the cabinet of curiosities, where they are still to be seen, provided they are not lost.

Was not this a lady of real delicacy?

THE REAL PRINCESS

Generalizations

B3 What generalizations can you make about the Prince, based on your list?

Classifications

B2 Classify your list into categories.

Details

B1 List the characteristics of the Prince.

Main Idea, Theme, or Concept

C3 Theme: What is the theme of this story?

Inference

C2 What evidence is there that the test was a good idea?

Literary Elements

C1 What kind of person is the Queen? How do you know?

One Girl's Song

By Susannah Wilson

I knew what the e-mail contained before I opened it. I knew as my mother, beaming, called, "Susannah! Come see what's on the computer before I open it myself!"

I knew as I stared at the nondescript subject line, willing my trembling hands to guide the cursor. I knew as I skimmed the insanely long paragraph, eyes snapping pass the meaningless "filler" sentences and hovering on "We regret that we are unable to accept you at this time . . ." Tears blurred the end of the sentence. I had known, but that didn't make it any less disappointing.

I pushed the screen away, got up resolutely, and went back to washing dishes. Wash, rinse, dry. Life couldn't come to a standstill because of a trivial rejection. But for some reason I couldn't wash them very efficiently. My whole body was still shaking. My mind scrolled through the empty, supposedly encouraging phrases that cushioned the cold, hard rejection. "Thank you for your interest in auditioning for the Texas honor choir . . . only one of many opportunities . . . it was a hard decision . . . as you know, we could only select a few . . ." I knew, all right. I had been secretly counting down to this date for weeks—months, even. I knew every detail about how the audition and acceptance process worked, having scoured the information pamphlet countless times.

I thought back to when I first recorded my audition with my dad. When he started the recorder, I would state my name (Susannah Wilson), age (12), and grade (seventh). He would walk to our piano and play a D. I would try to clear my mind except for the tips he had given me; then, with as much confidence as I could, I would sing my audition piece ("My Country, 'Tis of Thee"). After 20 minutes or so, my dad decided we were safe using one of the several recordings. I, still unsatisfied, said, "Just a few more, please, Daddy?" He gave in, and the next one I made was the one we kept.

After my audition was burned on the compact disc, I refused to listen to it. I couldn't stand to hear the sound of my own voice. It was so *immature*, and I could point out every flaw. My dad reminded me that nobody was perfect; there was nothing I could do to change my own humanity. My application was sent out, and I bit my nails to the quick. Some days I excitedly told my mother how fun the rehearsals and performances would be; most days I simply put down my attempt, saying there was no way I could make it in—there were *one thousand applicants*. However, something inside of me, maybe my pride, told me I *would* make it in. Even while cringing at the thought of the way my voice had broken, I knew I was going to be on the list. It was simply a matter of receiving that list, and that was taking entirely too long. But as I neared the date when I would I find out, I would catch myself thinking, "When I make it in . . ." and sternly scold myself: "*If*. *If* I make it." As the days crawled by, I tried to prepare myself for rejection. I guess I couldn't prepare myself enough.

Crying all over the clean dishes was enough of a nonverbal cue to bring my parents silently out to the kitchen, hugging me from behind and squeezing my shoulders, although I suspect my mom stopped to read the hated e-mail first.

They murmured words of encouragement and condolence and told me how proud they were. At first I said nothing, moving rigidly. Wash, rinse, dry. My mom said I didn't have to finish the dishes. I said I wanted to. When I eventually did, I broke down.

I don't even remember all that was exchanged between me and my parents. I was blubbering, I'm sure, pity-demanding words of self-deprecation. I do remember repeating, "I just wasn't good enough. They didn't want me."

"Susannah," said my dad. "You know they could only let in 50 altos. You very well could've been the 51st person on the judges' list."

"But that wasn't good enough! And I can't know that, anyway. I knew we should've recorded my audition one more time." My dad reached out and hugged me. "Daddy, I'm ruining your shirt," I sniffled.

"I don't care about that. Listen." He looked me in the eyes. "You were good enough to get into that choir." He had to say that, because he was my dad. But I believed him—a professional vocalist, greatest dad ever, and my sponsor for this audition. I probably had this easier than the 800 other kids who didn't make it.

But I couldn't let go of my emotions. "But if I was good enough, why didn't I get in?"

He sighed. "Susannah . . . I've judged this sort of thing before. You listen for tonal quality, the proper shaping of vowels, and of course pitch . . . but after a while they all sort of start to blur together. Sometimes it isn't easy to say, 'This person's the best, this person's second best, she's third best . . .' Sometimes there's a little bit of chance involved."

I stared at him, then at my mother, who was listening quietly. "But . . . that's not fair!" I said helplessly.

"Oh, sweetie," said my mom, coming toward me to hug me.

I scowled. "I'm still mad at the judges."

"I know," said my dad. "But please think about that when you feel better. They had a hard decision, I'm sure." Just like the e-mail. It had said, "Don't let this stop you from following your dreams." But I didn't want to take to heart anything said in the same message as, "We are unable to accept you at this time . . ."

"Okay," I said slowly. "But I'm never singing another note in my life."

"Please don't say that, Susannah."

I hadn't really meant it, though; I had said it somewhat halfheartedly. Later that day, I found myself humming "Stronger (What Doesn't Kill You)" by Kelly Clarkson.

"Well, I guess that applies," I thought sarcastically, "even though I'm pretty sure that song is about a break-up."

What doesn't kill you makes you stronger . . . stronger . . . And at that point I came to terms with the facts. I admitted to myself that I would not change the world by being in the choir. Nobody except me and my family would even care. To a member of the audience, one little girl's face and voice were easily interchangeable for another in a choir 200 strong. Sure, *I* would walk away changed. It would be a memorable experience. But I decided that I don't have to rely on anyone or anything to change myself. I can try again. Maybe next time, rejection will come a little easier. Or maybe next time, I'll accomplish what I set out to do.

Note. Originally published in *Creative Kids* magazine, Summer 2014. Reprinted with permission by Prufrock Press.

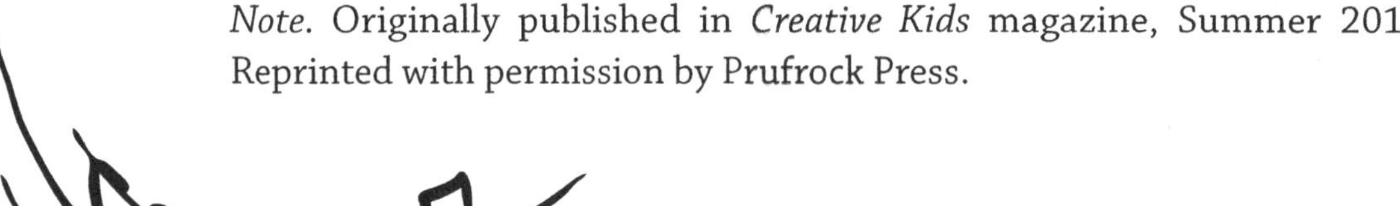

ONE GIRL'S SONG

Generalizations

B3 What generalizations can you make about the narrator, based on your reading?

Classifications

B2 Classify your list into categories.

Details

B1 List the characteristics of the author that you can discern from reading the story.

Creative Synthesis

D3 Pretend you are the narrator. On another sheet of paper, write a speech encouraging other students your age to participate in auditions or competitions.

Summarizing

D2 In five sentences or fewer, summarize what the narrator learned from the experience.

Paraphrasing

D1 In your own words, paraphrase the following quotation: "My dad reminded me that nobody was perfect; there was nothing I could do to change my own humanity."

The Three Spinning Fairies

By Jacob Grimm and Wilhelm Grimm

There was once upon a time a girl, who was lazy and hated work, and nothing her mother could say would induce her to spin. At last the mother grew angry, and losing all patience with her, gave her a beating. At this, the girl began to cry so loudly, that the queen who was driving past at the time, heard her cries and stopped.

She went into the house and asked the mother why she was beating her daughter like that; "her screams," she said, "can be heard outside in the street."

The mother was ashamed to confess the truth about her daughter's laziness, and so she answered:

"I cannot get her to leave off spinning; she is for ever at her wheel, and I am too poor to keep on buying her fresh flax."

"If that is all," said the queen, "there is nothing I like so much as the sound of spinning, and I am never happier than when I can hear the humming of the wheels; let me have your daughter, and I will take her home with me to the castle. I have plenty of flax, and she can go on spinning there to her heart's content."

The mother was heartily pleased at this proposal, and so the queen left, taking the girl with her. On their arrival at the castle, she took her upstairs and showed her three rooms, filled from floor to ceiling with the most beautiful flax.

"Spin me all this," said the queen, "and when it is finished, you shall have my eldest son for your husband; your poverty is not a matter of any consequence to me for I consider that your unremitting industry is an all sufficient dowry."

The girl dared not say anything, but she inwardly trembled with fear, for she knew that she could never spin all that flax, were she to sit at her spinning-wheel from morning till night for three hundred years. As soon as she was alone, she began to weep, and she sat like that for three days, without doing a stroke of work.

When the queen came again on the third day, she was surprised to find that the flax had not been touched. The girl excused herself by saying that she had felt so lonely and homesick, that she had not been able to begin her spinning. The queen was satisfied with this excuse, but as she was leaving, she said: "To-morrow, mind, I shall expect you to begin your work."

Alone once more, the girl was at her wits' end to know what to do, and in her distress of mind went and looked out of the window. There she saw three funny looking women coming towards her; one had a big flat foot, another a large under-lip that hung over her chin; and the third a very broad thumb. They stood still under the window, and looking up, asked the girl what was the matter. She told them her trouble, and they offered to help her. "If you will invite us to your wedding," they said, "and will not be ashamed of us, but introduce us as your cousins, and let us sit at your table, we will soon spin all that flax for you."

"That I will gladly promise," said the girl, "if you will but come in and begin working for me at once."

So she let in the three women, and queer little figures they looked; and cleared a space for them in the first room. They sat down and began their spinning; the first drew out the thread and turned the wheel, the second moistened the thread, and the third twisted it, striking with her fingers on the table, and every time she did this, a beautiful skein of the finest spun yarn fell on to the ground.

Whenever the queen came, the girl hid the three women, and then showed her skein upon skein of spun yarn, till the queen did not know how to find words enough to praise her.

As soon as the first room was empty, the spinners went on to the second, and finally to the third, which, like the others, was very quickly cleared of the flax. Then the three women took leave of the girl, saying to her as they parted, "Do not forget the promise you made us, for it will bring you good fortune." When the queen was shown the empty rooms and the great piles of yarn, she began at once to make preparations for the wedding. The bridegroom was delighted to think he should have such a clever and industrious wife, and showered his praises upon her.

"I have three cousins," said the girl, "and they have shown me such great kindness in the past, that I should not like to forget them, now that I am happy and prosperous. Will you give me permission to invite them to the wedding, and allow them to sit at our table?" The queen and the bridegroom both willingly consented to this request.

The wedding-feast was beginning when in walked the three women, attired in the most wonderful dresses. The bride greeted them, and said, "Welcome, dear cousins," but the bridegroom could not help exclaiming, "How came you to have such ugly friends."

Then he went up to the first, and asked her what had given her such a broad foot.

"Turning the wheel," she answered.

Then he went to the second, and asked what had caused her to have such a large lip.

"Moistening the thread," she answered.

Then he went on to the third, and asked what made her thumb so broad.

"Twisting the thread," she answered.

"Then," cried the prince, horrified at these answers, "my beautiful wife shall never go near a spinning-wheel again as long as she lives." And so, henceforth, she was rid of the hated task of spinning.

THE THREE SPINNING FAIRIES

Main Idea, Theme, or Concept

C3 Theme: A theme of this story is that sometimes individuals can be rewarded through trickery and deception. The Brothers Grimm wrote their stories more than 150 years ago, when cultural ideals might have been different than today. Is this theme one that would be acceptable today? Explain your answer.

Inference

C2 What inferences can you make about the prince? What evidence supports your answer?

Literary Elements

C1 How do the authors characterize the girl? Support your answer.

Creative Synthesis

D3 On another sheet of paper, rewrite this story in a modern setting. Change the theme from "sometimes individuals can be rewarded through trickery and deception" to one that has a positive message.

Summarizing

D2 In three sentences or fewer, summarize the message the authors were trying to give about people's appearance.

Paraphrasing

D1 In your own words, paraphrase the queen's statement: "your poverty is not a matter of any consequence to me for I consider that your unremitting industry is an all sufficient dowry."

9781618217363